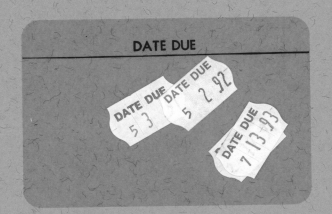

NEAR THE SEA

NEAR THE SEA

A PORTFOLIO OF PAINTINGS

JIM ARNOSKY

LOTHROP, LEE & SHEPARD BOOKS / NEW YORK

First Edition 1 2 3 4 5 6 7 8 9 10

Library of Congress Cataloging in Publication Data
Arnosky, Jim.
Near the sea : a portfolio of paintings / by Jim Arnosky.
p.   cm.   Summary: Provides paintings of beaches, rocks, water, gulls, fish, and other aspects of nature on
a small Maine island, accompanied by comments from the artist on how and why he painted them.
ISBN 0-688-08164-9. — ISBN 0-688-09327-2 (lib. bdg.)
1. Arnosky, Jim—Juvenile literature.   2. Maine in art—Juvenile literature.   3. Seashore in art—Juvenile literature.
[1. Seashore in art.   2. Animals in art.   3. Plants in art.   4. Maine in art.]
I. Title.   ND237.A745A4   1990   759.13—dc20   90-5722 CIP AC

This book is dedicated
to Les and Donna McNelly

INTRODUCTION

The paintings in this book all depict places on one small Maine island. It is an island connected to the mainland by a sturdy stone bridge that can be crossed in an automobile in less than a minute. Yet, once across, you are immediately aware that the island is very small and all around it churns the sea.

Last summer I spent two weeks roaming the island's outer edges, hiking over rocky shoreline, climbing steep coastal cliffs, seeking quiet deepwater coves, and exploring shallow tidal pools. I completed a painting a day, sometimes working rapidly in order to catch the curling of a wave as it occurred, or the changing shape of a gull winging overhead.

The first few days, beginning a painting at low tide, I found myself having to move my easel ever backward as the tide returned and flooded the land around me. Eventually, timing my outings according to the ebb and flow of the tide, I was able to work in the slow, sure, deliberate rhythm of life near the sea.

Jim Arnosky
RAMTAILS 1990

BLUEFISH

Soon after arriving on the island, I wandered down to the water's edge. There on a pile of rocks, a fisherman had left his morning catch— four large bluefish, so fresh that their colors had not yet begun to fade. I sketched the foursome just as they lay, making notes of the fishes' colors. As I worked, I imagined the fish still swimming in the sea, their mouths wide open, chasing after small mackerel.

Early next morning, the fisherman whose fish I had sketched invited me onto his boat to go fishing with him. We soon came upon schools of bluefish surface feeding, their dark dorsal fins and long, sharp tails poking up through the waves. We trolled large balsa-wood lures painted metallic colors so they would shine and flash in the water the way small baitfish do.

The bluefish struck our lures violently, imbedding the hooks in their mouths. Freshly hooked, bluefish dive. All we saw were our lines straining and being pulled through the water. After reeling the fish closer to the boat, we could see the fish down in the green water.

Just as we were about to boat a yard-long bluefish, a shark swam up from the depths and nosed in to see what our fish had in its mouth. The shark was a foot and a half longer than the bluefish. For a moment I thought it might try to steal the lure and we'd have two thrashing bodies to contend with. But the shark disappeared as suddenly as it had appeared, and in the next instant our captain, using a long pole with a sharp hook on the end, lifted the heavy bluefish out of the ocean.

CHANNEL

My day out on the ocean gave me a better sense of the island as a raised strip of land jutting up out of the water. An island is a mountain almost entirely submerged. Only the mountain top stands above the water. Around the mountain top are smaller, lower peaks and jutting ledges—reefs lurking unseen beneath the waves. Where two islands, each separate oceanic mountains, stand close together, the deep, flooded gorge between them is a channel connecting one section of open water to another.

The channel I painted is an important waterway, for it connects the sheltered bay and its safe harbors to the open ocean. Fishing vessels and lobster boats use the channel to get to and from their fishing waters. The channel is not marked with warning buoys or any other navigational aids. It is wide and deep and safe. Boats pass through at full throttle, sometimes two and three abreast. The channel is also a thoroughfare for fish. The fish use the channel for the same reason fishermen do: to travel back and forth from the sheltered waters of the bay to the open sea.

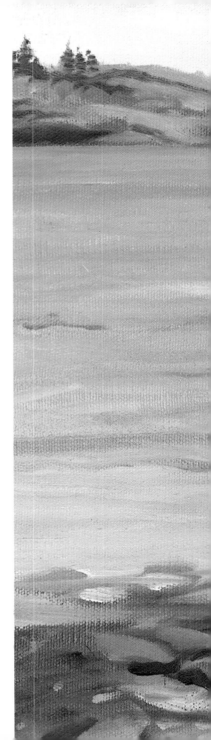

GULLS AND DRY ROCKS

In the late afternoon on a very hot day, the sun glowed pink through a dense haze. The sea and sky merged in the eye as one. Were it not for the faintly visible shapes of distant islands, I might have thought I was perched on some inland mountain top and not so near sea level.

Coastal Maine is rocky and rugged. You have to climb wherever you go. The rocks where I stood to paint this scene are high and dry, beyond the reach of the splashing and pounding of the waves, even at high tide. Gulls climb the breezes that blow over the rocks, pumping the air with their wings so powerfully that their bodies bob up and down with each stroke. And yet they make their travel look effortless. As they fly, they look this way and that, ever searching for something to eat.

Of all the birds, I most admire gulls. For their leisurely style of flight. For their sturdy shapes and bold yet simple markings. Most of all for the way they take a place and make it their own. Wherever gulls choose to land, on sea or shore, they belong.

12

OUTLAND

Along the seacoast there is a zone, an outland that, to my mind, can not be owned and thus belongs to everyone. It is the land the tide washes over. At low tide a person can wander there freely. But he must be careful not to slip and fall, for the outland is encrusted with millions of tiny barnacles sharp enough to cut through skin. All along the out- lands are slippery, seaweed-covered rocks. On the outland, at the edge of the grinding sea, I had to be especially aware of the ocean's cyclic ebb and flow, to avoid being stranded by an incoming tide.

During high tide, most of the outland is completely submerged. Waves pound and wear away the surfaces of boulders, cracking and cleaving them, shoving them around, picking them up and heaving them onto piles. Whole sections of ledge, slowly undermined by the sea, are eventually broken off and tipped up on end, so that their originally horizontal layers of sedimentary rock run vertically.

TIDAL POOL

As the tide recedes, shallow pools of salt water are left behind. Each tidal pool is a sunken treasure chest full of living jewels. Shiny blue-black mussels live all stuck together with attached barnacles, clams, fungi, and seaweeds. Alongside the mussel communities, green-spiked sea urchins huddle together.

When a sea urchin dies, it loses its spikes. Its insides wither until all that is left of the animal is a hollow oval globe of delicate purplish shell, all decorated with raised white dots. A tidal pool is littered with such remnants of life. Hermit crabs utilize empty moon shells and tiny conches by moving into them and adopting the shells as their own. There is a hermit crab in this painting and another crab—a rock crab with its own shell. The small sea snails are periwinkles. Periwinkles sometimes stick together, forming short charming chains.

Starfish are, to me, the most beautiful and fascinating of all tidal animals. Watch a starfish crawl over the bottom of a tidal pool. Its star-shaped body looks soft and pliant. See its smooth red eye. Is it looking at you? At a vertical rock the starfish begins to climb. Halfway up, it slips and tumbles down, landing on its back. The starfish rights itself in five slow steps, each leg doing its part. Again it attempts to scale the rock, reaching up and grasping the ledges, only to lose hold again. This time it changes its starry mind and crawls back toward the center of the pool.

16

COASTAL MARSH — LOW TIDE

When the tide goes out of the saltwater marshes connected to the sea, it seems to take all life with it, leaving only mud behind. The dull brown color of the tidal flats is a stark contrast to the glistening, vivid color in the seaside tidal pools. Walking around these drained places, I find no frogs hopping along the banks, snakes slithering in the reeds, or turtles sunning on driftwood logs—things only an inlander like myself would be on the lookout for.

But a saltwater marsh has its own denizens of grass, shore, and mud. Great blue herons and white egrets stalk the briny banks, hunting for mud and marsh crabs, picking tiny snails off the salted green blades, and spearing small fish stranded in the muddy puddles. The birds are not the only hunters on the marsh flats. When the tide is out, people come and dig for clams nestled down but not very deep in the mud.

At low tide you can better see how the land around a marsh just barely rises above the water's level at high tide. In this scene, even the little island in the center of the marsh shows actual land just barely above the water's highest level. It is the tall evergreens growing on the land that give the island height. Just beyond the evergreen island there is water—the limit of the low tide. Far off in the distance, where the water meets the sky, rests the sea.

18

COVE AND BOATYARD

I painted this scene at sundown. The late-day light cast a warm glow over the cove and boatyard. The island church bell was softly peeling a hymn to mark the end of another day and the tide was just beginning to flow back in.

The boatyard is old, rundown, and nearing the end of its usefulness. A large wooden sailboat, propped on steel-framed stands, was being overhauled. Its hull had been scraped and sanded. Cracks and gaps between the planking had been caulked. Some rotted timbers in the keel were being replaced. Only its rudder, propeller shaft, and propeller appeared to be shipshape. I would have liked to see the big boat finished and launched, its graceful form gently bobbing in the quiet water of the cove.

The cove is an ideal place to keep a boat. The water is deep enough, even during low tide, for a full-keeled boat to float without scraping the bottom. And because of the way the cove indents the coastline, its water is cradled on two sides by long arms of land—protection from even the strongest winds.

ASHORE

This view through growths of bittersweet, fireweed, and wild rose bushes is from the back lawn of a small shorefront cottage. I discovered it one morning while I was looking for a public right-of-way to the water across private property. I told a neighbor what I was doing there by the empty cottage and then set up my easel to begin what turned out to be a long day of painting.

People places, sheathed in shingles, gray from salt and sun, are perched all along this shore. They stand aloof, above the beach, just beyond the reach of the incoming tide. The ocean owns two-thirds of this round earth and would have the rest inch by inch. At high tide, when the water crashes in on this shore, it splashes up and sends a spray that salts the green lawns and flower gardens.

Although I was working on a shore lined with comfortable summer homes, I imagined I had been set ashore on a wild deserted isle, and was happy to be stranded.

THE SURF

Down on a long lonely stretch of beach, an hour or so before high tide, the surf was rushing in, splashing and foaming over stones. A pair of sandpipers flew over the water. It is amazing how the birds can fly so fast and low, so near the breaking waves, without getting splashed. Perhaps they do! I'm sure they felt the ocean's spray. I could feel it where I was standing.

After a few hours painting the incoming surf, you begin to sense the rhythm of the waves—first a series of small waves, then others slightly larger, followed by the roaring forms of great big waves, each in its turn breaking on the shore.

Watch a great wave taking shape beyond the surf. A moving mass of energy raises a ridge of water surface that swells as it gains momentum, building to a white-capped wedge, then cresting in a great curving arc of water, luminous, sparkling, hurling itself toward the shore. As the roaring wall of water advances, one end of the arc curls forward and rolls over, forming a funneling, moving mouth of water that would swallow the entire wave if the whole shebang did not break and come crashing splashing down.

24

CLIFF AND SEA

Sailors watch the wind and its effects on the surface of the water to gauge the degrees of danger the sea presents. They speak of calm seas, fair seas, lively seas, threatening seas. To a seafarer threatening seas ascend a ladder of alarm ranging in wind strength and speed from near-gale to gale to hurricane force. But as dangerous as strong winds and gigantic offshore waves may be, most shipwrecks do not occur on the open sea. Maritime wrecks most often occur near land, where a wayward ship can run aground in a storm or a fair-weather fog and be smashed against the rocks.

From this place up on the edge of a steep cliff, the sea below looks dangerous and it is. A boat or body cast into the churning water would be drowned and ground against the submerged rocks. The cliff is a natural formation of giant steps. At high tide, the pounding surf rushes up the rocky steps and leaps high over the ground.

While I was painting the cliff and sea, an islander stopped to watch and chat. She told me that in her youth she had seen this place during a hurricane. With each tremendous wave, the sea shot straight up into the air like a geyser. "What a roar!" she exclaimed. "What a frightening roar!" And as she spoke her whole body shook from the memory.

BEACH

This short length of beach is about as much as the islands' rocky coast allows, and the sand is quite coarse. There are no really fine grains, only broken bits of shell and stone and bottle glass—some pieces large enough to allow light to shine through them, at times making the beach glitter as if it were strewn with gemstones. There are many smooth, rounded pebbles in the mix, and some miniature, unbroken shells. I found one bright orange conch no bigger than a pea.

As I painted the beach on the last day of my stay, the afternoon sky became overcast. The wind began to blow. The air became unseasonably cold. I was exhilarated by the change of weather. I had had my fill of sunny, hot, hazy days and warm breezes. The color of the waves deepened to a dark metallic blue. There were no shadows; the beach took on a somber tone. The only birds were killdeer the colors of the sand and seashells. They foraged along the water's edge for morsels of food amid the washed-in weeds, shells, driftwood, and chunks of broken boards.

I painted through the afternoon, for as long as I could stand the wind and ignore the hunger growling in my stomach. Then I folded my easel, picked up my belongings, and left the beach and the island and the sea.

28

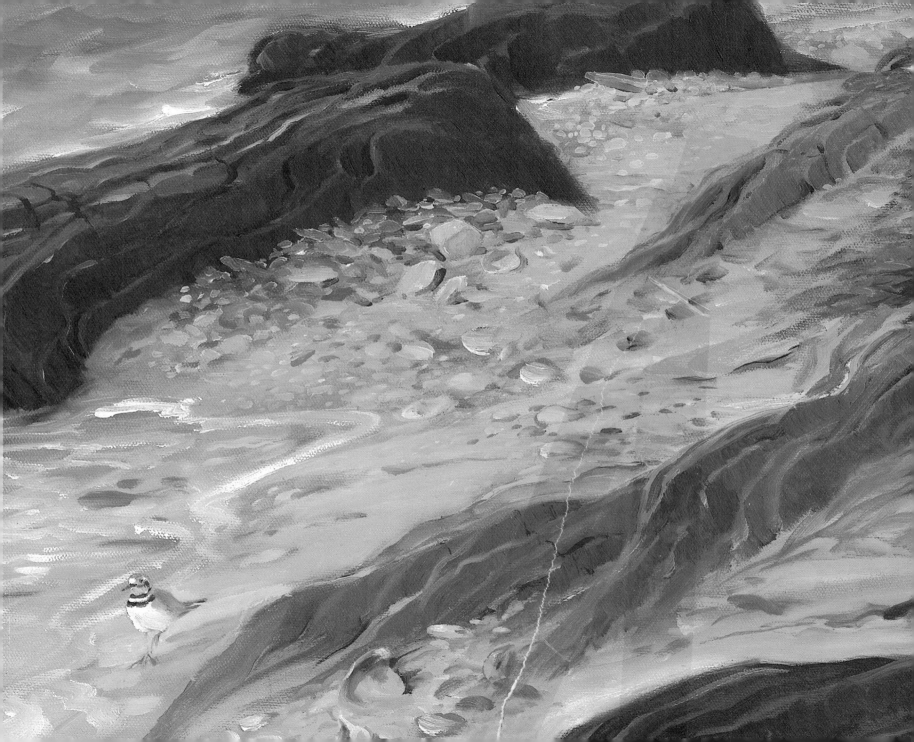

Paintings executed in oils on canvas. To economize on weight carried while hiking,
Mr. Arnosky limited his palette to six colors: red, light yellow, yellow ochre,
permanent blue, raw umber, and white.

Designed by Jim Arnosky.
Typography and layout by Cindy Simon. Composed by Pulsar Graphics in
12 pt. ITC Novarese Book.

Color separations by Accent on Color.
Printed on Sterling Litho Satin Matte paper by General Offset Company, Inc.